# Chrismons —
## They Point To Jesus

### Diane L. Gibson

CSS Publishing Company, Inc., Lima, Ohio

CHRISMONS — THEY POINT TO JESUS

Reprinted 2002

Copyright © 1996 by
CSS Publishing Company, Inc.
Lima, Ohio

The original purchaser may photocopy material in this publication for use as it was intended (i.e., worship material for worship use; educational material for classroom use; dramatic material for staging or production). No additional permission is required from the publisher for such copying by the original purchaser only. Inquiries should be addressed to: Permissions, CSS Publishing Company, Inc., P.O. Box 4503, Lima, Ohio 45802-4503.

Scripture quotations are from the *Holy Bible, New International Version.* Copyright © 1973, 1978, 1984 International Bible Society. Used by permission of Zondervan Bible Publishers. All rights reserved.

For more information about CSS Publishing Company resources, visit our website at www.csspub.com or e-mail us at custserv@csspub.com or call (800) 241-4056.

ISBN 0-7880-0849-8                    PRINTED IN U.S.A.

*For the "Crafters" at Calvary Lutheran Church*
*for the loving way in which they made numerous Chrismons*
*to grace our sanctuary Christmas tree.*

# Table Of Contents

# Order Of Worship

## *Chrismons — They Point To Jesus*

Prelude

Processional Hymn: "O Come, All Ye Faithful"

**Invitation To Worship:**
> Leader: In the name of the Father, and of the Son, and of the Holy Spirit.
> **Cong: Amen.**
> Leader: We come to give glory to the Father, the Author of our salvation.
> **Cong: We come to give glory to the Son, who came in the flesh to be our Savior.**
> Leader: We come to give glory to the Spirit, who sustains us in the faith.
> **All: Glory be to You, O Lord. We come to worship You!**

**The Message**

**The Offering**

**Song:** "Ding Dong! Merrily On High" (alt. "Of The Father's Love Begotten")

**Scene I:** What Are Chrismons?

**Scene II:** The Hand (God The Father)

**Hymn:** "Alleluia! Let Praises Ring" (alt. "Come, Thou Almighty King")

**Scene III:** The Holy Trinity

**Hymn:** "Holy, Holy, Holy"

**Scene IV:** The Creator's Star

**Scene V:** The Angel

**Song:** "Angels Came From Heaven" (alt. "Baby Jesus")

**Song:** "Emmanuel, Emmanuel" (alt. "Angels We Have Heard On High")

**Scene VI:** The Manger

**Song:** "Away In A Manger"

**Scene VII:** The Chi-Rho (Christ)

**Scene VIII:** The Fish (Jesus Our Savior)

**Song:** "Alleluia" (alt. "Good Christian Men, Rejoice")

**Scene IX:** The Crown Of Thorns

**Hymn:** "When I Survey The Wondrous Cross"

**Scene X:** The Cross (The Latin Cross, The Jerusalem Cross, and The Cross Fleurie)

**Hymn:** "Lift High The Cross"

**Scene XI:** The Butterfly (Resurrection)

**Hymn:** "Christ The Lord Is Risen Today"

**Scene XII:** The Crown

**Hymn:** "Crown Him With Many Crowns"

**Scene XIII:** The Dove And The Flame (The Holy Spirit)

**Hymn:** "Holy Spirit, Light Divine"

**Scene XIV:** The Word (The Lamp And The Candle)

**Hymn:** "O Word Of God Incarnate"

**Scene XV:** The Shell (Our Baptism)

**Scene XVI:** The Chalice (Holy Communion)

**Hymn:** "O Jesus, Blessed Lord, My Praise" (alt. "Jesus, Thy Blood
And Righteousness)

**Scene XVII:** The Chrismons Summarize Our Christian Life

**Scene XVIII:** Always Be Thankful (Our Response)

**Song:** "Thank You, Lord" (alt. "Holy God, We Praise Thy Name")

**Song:** "Were You There On That Christmas Night?" *(may be omitted)*

**Recessional Hymn:** "Joy To The World"

# *Chrismons —*
# *They Point To Jesus*
## by Diane L. Gibson

**Setting:** A church sanctuary

**Props:** A Christmas tree decorated with Chrismons. Twenty poster board banners, each depicting a large Chrismon.

**Characters:** An adult, first child, second child, various speakers

✠ ✠ ✠ ✠ ✠

**Prelude**

**Processional Hymn:** "O Come, All Ye Faithful"

**Invitation to Worship:**
Leader:  In the name of the Father, and of the Son, and of the Holy Spirit.
**Cong:  Amen.**
Leader:  We come to give glory to the Father, the Author of our salvation.
**Cong:  We come to give glory to the Son, who came in the flesh to be our Savior.**
Leader:  We come to give glory to the Spirit, who sustains us in the faith.
**All:  Glory be to You, O Lord. We come to worship You!**

**The Message**

**The Offering**

**Song:** "Ding Dong! Merrily On High" (alt. "Of The Father's Love Begotten")

### Scene I — *What Are Chrismons?*

**First Child:** What a beautiful tree! Those ornaments are really pretty!

**Second Child:** They are different than any ornaments I've seen before.

**Adult:** The ornaments are called Chrismons. They are all Christian symbols that give honor to Christ.

**First Child:** Why are they called Chrismons?

**Adult:** "Chrismons" actually comes from two words: "Christ" and "monogram." A Chrismon is just that — a monogram of Christ.

**Second Child:** What's a monogram?

**Adult:** Have you ever put your initials on one of your school items or on a sweater or jacket?

**First Child:** I have. My initials are "L.E.C." That stands for Lauren Elizabeth Carter.

**Adult:** Well, that's what a monogram is. If we made a monogram for Jesus today we might write: "J.C." to stand for "Jesus Christ." But in Jesus' time they didn't write in English. They wrote in Greek. Some of the ornaments on the tree are like Greek initials for the words for Jesus and Christ, and so on.

**Second Child:** But not all the ornaments on the trees are letters.

12

**Adult:** You're absolutely right! Sometimes we remember things better if we see a picture or symbol. From the earliest times people drew different pictures or symbols to help explain what they believed about God. In fact, many of these symbols were designed almost 2000 years ago by the first Christians. They put them on their door posts, utensils, and catacombs to make a statement about what they believed. Many have remained until today and you see them now as Chrismons on our tree.

**First Child:** I see. So they all point to God and tell something about Him. We can learn more about Him just by studying these ornaments.

**Second Child:** But why are they all only white and gold?

**Adult:** White is the liturgical color for Christmas. It refers to the Lord's purity and perfection. Several scripture references describe God with the color "white." At Jesus' transfiguration his clothes became dazzling white. In the book of Revelation it says Jesus will appear on a great white throne appearing white like wool and snow.

**First Child:** What about the gold?

**Adult:** Gold points to God's glory and majesty. God instructed that much of His temple be overlaid with gold. Heaven is described as having streets of gold, and Jesus is described as wearing a golden sash when He appears in all His glory.

**Second Child:** I'd like to learn about what all these symbols mean.

**First Child:** Me, too. May we?

**Adult:** Yes, of course. When we do, we can give glory to God. And that's the real reason for celebrating Christmas!

## Scene II —*The Hand (God The Father)*

**Speaker 1:** A hand is used to symbolize God the Father. There are many verses that speak of God in terms of a hand.

**Speaker 2:** God the Father is shown as the Creator by this verse from Isaiah 48:13: "My own hand laid the foundation of the earth, and my right hand spread out the heavens."

**Speaker 3:** His hand also shows His protection over us. Psalm 139:10 says: "Your hand will guide me, your right hand will hold me fast."

**Speaker 4:** Many different positions of the hand are used to symbolize God the Father. This is the Latin form. The three fingers pointing up represent the three persons of the Trinity. *(Point to the thumb and first two fingers.)* The two closed fingers show the twofold nature of Jesus. He was both God and man. *(Point to the two small, closed fingers.)*

**Speaker 5:** The circle around it is a nimbus. The nimbus is a sign of sanctity. This means God is holy. The three rays within it represent the deity of God. This means He is supreme and powerful.

**Speaker 6:** Some pastors hold their hands in this position as they give the benediction at the end of the service. That's because they are pronouncing God's blessing on us.

**Hymn:** "Alleluia! Let Praises Ring" (alt. "Come, Thou Almighty King")

## Scene III — *The Holy Trinity*

**Speaker 1:** This is the symbol for the Holy Trinity. God is one God, but there are three persons: the Father, the Son, and the Holy Spirit.

**Speaker 2:** We know there are three persons in the Trinity from God's Word in Matthew 28:19: "Go and make disciples of all nations, baptizing them in the name of the Father and of the Son and of the Holy Spirit."

**Speaker 3:** There are many symbols used to show the Trinity. This one uses an equilateral triangle. All three sides are of equal length and its three angles are identical. This shows the equality of the three persons of God. But all three sides join together to form one figure. This shows the unity of the Trinity.

**Speaker 4:** Here the triangle is overlaid with a trefoil. A trefoil is like three interwoven circles with the overlapping parts cut out. The three circles indicate the three persons of the Trinity. They are combined into one figure to show that they are one God.

**Hymn:** "Holy, Holy, Holy"

## Scene IV — *The Creator's Star*

**Speaker 1:** This is called the Creator's Star. God the Father created the world in six days. That is why the star has six points. *(Speaker points to each point as he counts all six.)*

**Speaker 2:** If you follow my finger you can see how this star is formed by joining two triangles together. Here is one triangle: *(traces first triangle with finger)* and here is the second triangle. *(Traces second triangle.)*

**Speaker 3:** All three persons of the Trinity were present at the creation of the world, even though it was the work of God the Father to create it.

**Speaker 4:** Some have also used the six points of this star to refer to six attributes of God the Father: power, wisdom, majesty, love, mercy, and justice.

## Scene V — *The Angel*

*This scene is carried out as a chapel talk with the youngest children (nursery, preschool, or kindergarten age). Two speakers address questions to the children who are gathered around them.*

16

**Speaker 1:** Now we will look at several symbols that especially remind us of Christmas. When it was time for Jesus to be born. God sent someone to tell Mary that she would be the mother of Jesus.

**Speaker 2:** Do you know who told Mary that she would be Jesus' mother?

(*Children respond with:* "An angel" *or* "The angel, Gabriel.")

What words do you think the angel said to Mary? *(Allow for responses.)*

How do you think Mary felt? (Allow for responses.)

Were there any other angels in the Christmas story? *(Allow for responses concerning the pronouncement to Joseph and/or the shepherds.)*

What did the angel say to the shepherds? *(Allow for responses.)*

**Speaker 1:** Then many, many angels appeared in the sky. What did they do? What words did they sing? *(Allow for responses.)*

Do you think you could sing like the angels? Let's try.

**Song:** "Angels Came From Heaven" (Tune: "In a Little Stable")

Angels came from heaven
Down to earth below
Bringing us the message
We are glad to know.

Jesus Christ the Savior
He is born today.
You will find Him sleeping
Softly on the hay.

"Glory in the highest"
Were the words they sang.
"Peace on earth to all men"
Hear the glad refrain.

17

"Baby Jesus" (Tune: "Frère Jacques")
Baby Jesus, Baby Jesus,
Born today, born today.
You came down from heaven.
You came down from heaven.
I love You. I love You.

Baby Jesus, Baby Jesus,
You're my King, You're my King.
Thank you, Lord, for coming.
Thank you, Lord, for coming.
I love You. I love You.

Baby Jesus, Baby Jesus,
Born today, born today.
Glory in the Highest.
Glory in the Highest.
A-men. A-men.

**Song:** "Emmanuel, Emmanuel" (alt. "Angels We Have Heard On High")

### Scene VI — *The Manger*
*This scene is also carried out as a chapel talk. You may use a second group of your youngest children.*

**Speaker 1:** Our Jesus was born. What a wonderful day! God sent us a Savior to take away our sins and give us eternal life. What a gift!

**Speaker 2:** Our next symbol shows us how God sent us a Savior.
*(To children)* Can you tell us where Jesus was born? *(Allow for responses.)*
Yes. He was born in a manger in Bethlehem. This is the symbol we use for the manger.
*(Point to the symbol on the poster.)* Do you know what a manger is used for? *(Allow for responses.)*
Why do you suppose God had Jesus born here? *(Allow for responses.)*
Jesus became a baby just like you and me. He wasn't proud. He knows all about us because he became a man for us.

**Speaker 1:** Do you see this circle on top of the manger? Do you know what it means? *(Allow for responses)*
Yes, it stands for Jesus. It's called a nimbus. Can you say that? It means that Jesus is holy. He never does anything wrong. He never sins. That's how Jesus is different than we are. That's what makes Him God. He had to be perfect to take away our sins.
Do you know any songs about baby Jesus in the manger? Could you sing one to Him now?

**Song:** "Away In A Manger "

## Scene VII — *The Chi-Rho (Christ)*

19

**Speaker 1:** There are many symbols that point us to Jesus. One of the most common symbols is the Chi-Rho. The letters "X" and "P" are joined together to form a monogram like we talked about earlier.

**Speaker 2:** "X" and "P" are the first two letters of the Greek word for Christ: Christos (XPICTOC).

**Speaker 3:** The Greek letters X and P are pronounced "Chi-Rho."

**Speaker 4:** Now every time I see this symbol I know that it stands for Christ.

### Scene VIII — *The Fish (Jesus Our Savior)*

**Speaker 1:** The fish is one of the most ancient symbols for the Savior.

**Speaker 2:** Often the Greek word, "IXOYC," *(pronounced ichthus)* meaning "fish" was written alongside it. Each letter in this word was used to form a rebus which meant "Jesus Christ, Son of God, Savior." This was like a little sermon in stone for the Christians. It expressed their need for a Savior, and the fact that salvation comes only through Jesus Christ.

**Speaker 3:** Early Christians often used this as a secret sign. When it appeared outside a Christian home, it was a sign that the Lord's Supper would be celebrated there, that night, in secret.

**Song:** "Alleluia!" (alt. "Good Christian Men, Rejoice")

20

## Scene IX — *The Crown Of Thorns*

**Speaker 1:** The crown of thorns is a passion symbol indicating our suffering Savior.

**Speaker 2:** It reminds us of the mocking and pain Jesus endured as the Roman soldiers put a scarlet robe on Him and then twisted together a crown of thorns for his head.

**Speaker 3:** The crown is shown with three nails to indicate the nails that were used to hang Jesus to the cross at his hands and feet.

**Speaker 4:** This symbol shows only the beginning of the suffering Jesus endured to take away our sins.

**Hymn:** "When I Survey The Wondrous Cross"

### Scene X — *The Cross (The Latin Cross, The Jerusalem Cross, And The Cross Fleurie)*

**Speaker 1:** The cross is the greatest symbol of the Christian church. Without Jesus' death on the cross, we would be lost forever. Since the cross carries such great significance, over 400 forms of the cross have been designed.

**Speaker 2:** Of these, about 50 have been used in Christian symbolism. We will show you three different types of crosses today.

21

**Speaker 3:** The Latin cross, also sometimes called the Roman cross, is the most common of all the crosses. It is on this cross that Jesus was crucified.

**Speaker 4:** This cross is recognized throughout the world by those who confess Jesus Christ as their Lord and Savior, who died for them on the cross.

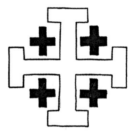

**Speaker 5:** This is the Jerusalem cross or Crusader's cross. This cross has come to mean many things. The center cross is made by joining four Tau crosses. Tau crosses represent the Old Testament prophecies of a Savior. The four smaller crosses represent the four Gospels which have displaced the Mosaic Law represented by the Tau crosses.

**Speaker 6:** Others say that the five crosses represent the five wounds our Lord suffered at the crucifixion.

**Speaker 7:** The Jerusalem Cross has also been interpreted as signifying Christian missions, the large cross standing for the early Christian Church at Jerusalem and the four small Greek crosses signifying the four corners of the earth.

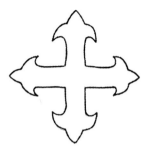

**Speaker 8:** This is the cross Fleurie, which is French for "flowery." Its ends resemble the petals of a flower. It is a beautiful form of the cross, embellished for use in many church decorations. Sometimes we make the cross beautiful because of the beautiful way God showed His love for us by his death on the cross.

**Hymn:** "Lift High the Cross"

### Scene XI — *The Butterfly (Resurrection)*

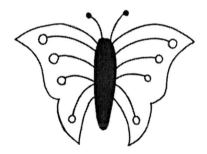

**Speaker 1:** Jesus' work was not finished when He died for us on the cross. He did not stay in the tomb but burst forth alive on Easter Day. The victory of His resurrection is shown by the butterfly.

**Speaker 2:** Just like a seemingly lifeless chrysalis bursts forth into a beautiful new butterfly, so did Jesus' lifeless body burst forth from the tomb into a victorious resurrected life.

**Speaker 3:** The life cycle of the butterfly is like our own lives as well. The larva can be compared to our lowly sinful bodies. The chrysalis is like our bodies in the grave. And the butterfly symbolizes the glorious bodies we will have someday when we receive eternal life.

**Hymn:** "Christ The Lord Is Risen Today"

### Scene XII — *The Crown*

**Speaker 1:** The crown symbolizes Jesus as our King. He is the King of kings and Lord of lords. He rules over the heavens and the earth.

**Speaker 2:** The crown also reminds us that someday we will also receive the crown of life when we go to heaven.

**Speaker 3:** Revelation 2:10 says: "Be faithful, even to the point of death, and I will give you the crown of life."

**Hymn:** "Crown Him With Many Crowns"

## Scene XIII — *The Dove And The Flame (The Holy Spirit)*

**Speaker 1:** When Jesus ascended into heaven as our Resurrected King, he did not leave us alone. He sent the Holy Spirit to live in our hearts and guide us in our faith and life.

**Speaker 2:** The most common symbol for the Holy Spirit is the dove. This symbol originated from Jesus' baptism when the Holy Spirit descended upon Him as a dove.

**Speaker 3:** The dove is shown with a three-rayed nimbus. The three rays symbolize the Deity of God. The nimbus is a symbol of sanctity, showing the holiness of God.

**Speaker 4:** If you will notice, the dove is shown in a descending form. He comes from heaven down to earth to live among us.

**Speaker 5:** Another symbol for the Holy Spirit is the flame of fire. On Pentecost tongues of fire rested on the heads of the disciples. They were filled with the Holy Spirit and began to speak in other tongues.

**Hymn:** "Holy Spirit, Light Divine"

25

## Scene XIV — *The Word (The Lamp And The Candle)*

**Speaker 1:** God's Holy Word is depicted in several ways. Many times it is symbolized with an open book. Sometimes it is also symbolized by a lamp.

**Speaker 2:** This symbolism stems from the words of Psalm 119:105 which say: "Your word is a lamp to my feet and a light for my path."

**Speaker 3:** The candle also symbolizes the Word as it lights our way and shows us the Truth.

**Hymn:** "O Word Of God Incarnate"

## Scene XV — *The Shell (Our Baptism)*

26

**Speaker 1:** God brings us to faith through our baptism. The shell is a symbol for baptism since it reminds us of the water used when we are baptized in the name of the Father, and of the Son, and of the Holy Spirit.

**Speaker 2:** When we see a shell we can be reminded of the miracle of God making us His children through this holy sacrament.

### Scene XVI — *The Chalice (Holy Communion)*

**Speaker 1:** The usual symbol for the Lord's Supper is a chalice with a host or wafer rising out of it.

**Speaker 2:** Sometimes the letters I.N.R.I. or IHC are imprinted on the wafer. This symbolizes the Real Presence in, with, and under the bread and wine.

**Speaker 3:** Jesus said: "Take, eat, this is my body. Take, drink, this is my blood. Do this in remembrance of Me."

**Hymn:** "O Jesus, Blessed Lord, My Praise" (alt. "Jesus, Thy Blood And Righteousness")

### Scene XVII — *The Chrismons Summarize Our Christian Life*
*Return to the front the following Chrismons, assembled in this order: the shell, the hand of God, the Chi-Rho, the dove, the Latin cross, the lamp, the chalice, the butterfly, the crown*

**Speaker 1:** As we look back over some of the Chrismons we have seen, we can see that they summarize for us our life in Christ.

**Speaker 2:** Through Holy Baptism, *(point to shell)*, in the name of the Father *(point to the hand)*, and of the Son *(point to the Chi-Rho)*, and of the Holy Spirit *(point to the dove)*, we are brought to faith in Jesus, our Lord and Savior, who redeemed us by His death on the cross *(point to the Latin cross)*. Through His Word *(point to the lamp)* and the sacrament of Holy Communion *(point to the chalice)* we are strengthened, until that great day when we shall rise to eternal life *(point to the butterfly)* and see our great Lord and Savior, the King of Kings *(point to the crown)*.

### Scene XVIII — *Always Be Thankful (Our Response)*

**Speaker 1:** What blessings we have received from our Lord and Savior! We can only respond with hearts of joy and thankfulness! That is why we conclude with one last Chrismon — a picture of ourselves as kneeling servants always being thankful to God for what He has done.

**Song:** "Thank You, Lord" (alt. "Holy God, We Praise Thy Name")

**Song:** "Were You There On That Christmas Night?" (may be omitted)

**Recessional Hymn:** "Joy To The World"

28

# Directions For
# Making Chrismons

Chrismons may be made as simply or as elaborately as you desire. All Chrismons include only the colors white and gold. Suggestions are given for the placement of these two colors on the patterns. You may vary the color placement as well as the type of ornamentation you use, according to your own imagination. The patterns may also be enlarged or made smaller, depending on the size of your tree.

**Chrismons made by children:**
If made by children, use of white poster board or white styrofoam is suggested. (Styrofoam meat trays obtained from a grocery store work best.) Place the pattern over the surface and trace, cutting the outline with an Exacto knife, razor blade, or scissors. Gold features may be added with gold glitter or sequins. (Patterns may be photocopied, cut out, and glued onto the poster board or styrofoam. This will make it easier for the children to know where to add gold glitter.) Add gold cord or thread to hang.

Author's note: In our church, we wanted to involve all the children in this project. Since the very youngest children could not handle all the tracing and cutting, we assigned junior high and high school age children to do a lot of this work for the younger grades. After making the basic Chrismon shapes, this older age group went into the classrooms to help the children add glitter to their Chrismons.

**Chrismons made by adults:**

Chrismons made by adults may include any white fabric or felt, with ornamentation added using white or gold beads, sequins, ornamental pins or stars, ribbon, and braid. A front and back side may be cut of each ornament. After the front side is decorated, it may be sewn to the back and stuffed with polyester batting to give it depth and firmness.

If you want your Chrismons to last for many years, we suggest sewing on the individual sequins, beads, braid, or other ornamentation you are using. Sequins, especially, tend to flake off with abrasion. You will be much more pleased with your Chrismons if you take the extra time to sew on the trimmings.

Chrismons that have non-connecting parts or thin cross bars may be mounted on a circular or rectangular background of white fabric, i.e., the Jerusalem cross, the Chi-Rho, the fish, or the chalice.

# Displaying The Chrismons On Posterboard For The Program

For the program itself, we knew that the Chrismons were too small to be seen clearly by those in the audience or congregation. To solve this problem we copied the line drawings of the Chrismons onto an overhead transparency. We projected each Chrismon symbol onto white butcher paper using an overhead transparency machine. We enlarged each one to approximately 15" in diameter. We traced the Chrismons, cut them out, and mounted each one onto a red sheet of posterboard. Each group of children was responsible for decorating these Chrismons with gold glitter.

Using a glue gun, we mounted a lath strip (a length approximately 18" longer than the length of the posterboard) down the center of the back of each posterboard. This allowed each posterboard to be carried like a banner by each of the children. As each Chrismon was explained, its corresponding posterboard banner was also displayed, and then paraded throughout the sanctuary or auditorium so all could clearly see it. (The actual Chrismon ornaments were displayed on a tree at the front of the sanctuary.)

# Bibliography

Koch, Rudolf, *The Book of Signs*, Dover Publications, Inc., New York, NY, 10014, 1955.

Post, W. Ellwood, *Saints, Signs, and Symbols*, Morehouse-Barlow Co., Wilton, CT, 1974.

Spencer, Frances Kipps, *Chrismons*, © 1970 by The Evangelical Lutheran Church of the Ascension, Danville, VA, McCain Printing, Danville, VA.
The Lutheran Church of the Ascension
314 West Main Street
Danville, Virginia 24541
(Patterns and instructions for making Chrismons are available by writing the church indicated above.)

Stafford, Thomas Albert, *Christian Symbolism in the Evangelical Churches*, Abingdon Press, Nashville, TN, MCMXLII.

Suffling, Ernest, R., *Church Festival Decorations*, Gale Research Co., Book Tower, Detroit, MI, 1974.

Webber, F.R., *Church Symbolism*, Gale Research Co., Book Tower, 1971.

Wetzler, Robert and Helen Huntington, *Seasons and Symbols, a Handbook on the Church Year*, Augsburg Publishing House, Minneapolis, MN, 55440, 1962.

# Acknowledgments
# Of Lesser Known Songs

*Introduction*
"Ding Dong! Merrily On High"
Text: Patricia Lou Harris
Arrangement: from a traditional French carol
Copyright © MCMXCII, Kirkland House. Division of The Lorenz
   Corp., Dayton, OH 45401

*Scene II*
"Alleluia! Let Praises Ring"
Text: author unknown
Tune: Philipp Nicolai, 1556-1608
Setting: *Lutheran Worship*
Copyright © 1982, Concordia Publishing House, St. Louis, MO

*Scene III*
"Holy, Holy, Holy"
Text: Reginald Heber
Tune: John B. Dykes
Setting: *Lutheran Worship*
Copyright © 1982, Concordia Publishing House, St. Louis, MO

*Scene V*
"Angels Came From Heaven"
Text: Diane L. Gibson
Tune: E.W. Schroeter
Setting: *Little Ones Sing Praise*
Copyright © 1989, Concordia Publishing House, St. Louis, MO

"Baby Jesus"
Text: Diane Gibson
Tune: Traditional

"Emmanuel, Emmanuel"
Text and Tune: Charles F. Brown
Setting: *Sing 'n' Celebrate for Kids*
Copyright © 1977, Word Inc., Waco, TX 76703

*Scene VIII*
"Alleluia!"
Text and Tune: Terry Kirkland
Setting: *It's Christmas! A Christmas Cantata for Children*
Copyright © MCMLXXXVIII, Kirkland House, Box 802, Dayton, OH 45401

*Scene IX*
"When I Survey The Wondrous Cross"
Text: Isaac Watts
Tune: Lowell Mason
Setting: *Lutheran Worship*
Copyright © 1982, Concordia Publishing House, St. Louis, MO

*Scene X*
"Lift High the Cross"
Text: George W. Kitchin
Tune:  Sydney H. Nicholson
Setting: *Lutheran Worship*
Copyright © 1982, Concordia Publishing House, St. Louis, MO

*Scene XI*
"Christ The Lord Is Risen Today"
Text: Charles Wesley
Tune: French, 13th century
Setting: *Lutheran Worship*
Copyright © 1982, Concordia Publishing House, St. Louis, MO

*Scene XII*
"Crown Him With Many Crowns"
Text: Matthew Bridges, Godfre Thring
Tune: George J. Elvey
Setting: *Lutheran Worship*
Copyright © 1982, Concordia Publishing House, St. Louis, MO

*Scene XIII*
"Holy Spirit, Light Divine"
Text: Andrew Reed, Samuel Longfellow
Tune: Orlando Gibbons
Setting: *Lutheran Worship*
Copyright © 1982, Concordia Publishing House, St. Louis, MO

*Scene XIV*
"O Word Of God Incarnate"
Text: William W. How
Tune: Neu-vermehrtes Gesangbuch, Meiningen
Setting: *Lutheran Worship*
Copyright © 1982, Concordia Publishing House, St. Louis, MO

*Scene XVI*
"O Jesus, Blessed Lord, My Praise"
Text: Thomas H. Kingo, tr. Arthur J. Mason
Tune: Louis Bourgeois
Setting: *Lutheran Worship*
Copyright © 1982, Concordia Publishing House, St. Louis, MO

*Scene XVIII*
"Thank You, Lord"
Text and Tune: Traditional
Arr. Copyright © 1986 New Spring Publishing
Setting: *Kids Sing Praise*
Brentwood Music, Brentwood, TN 37027

"Were You There On That Christmas Night?"
Text and Tune: Natalie Sleeth
Copyright © 1976, Hope Publishing Co.

**The Hand Of God
(God The Father)**

**The Trinity**

**The Creator's Star**

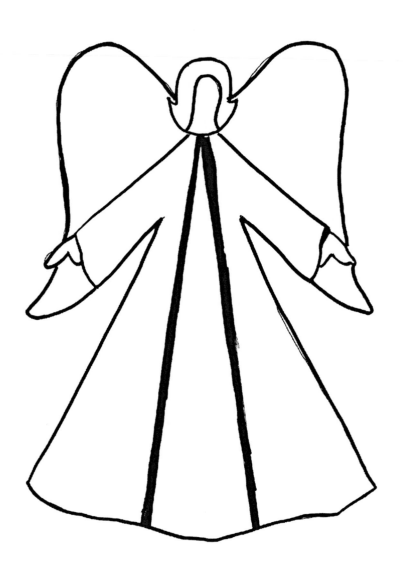

**The Angel**

**The Manger**

41

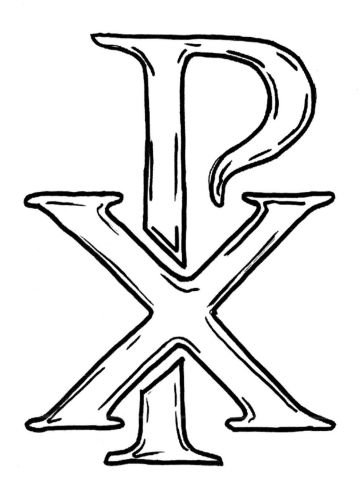

**The Chi-Rho**
**(Christ)**

42

**The Fish**
**(Jesus Our Savior)**

43

**The Crown Of Thorns**

44

**The Latin Cross**

**The Jerusalem Cross**

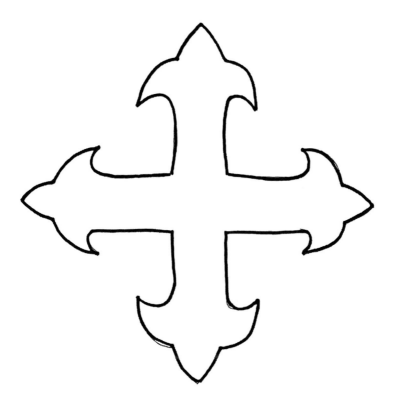

**The Cross Fleurie**

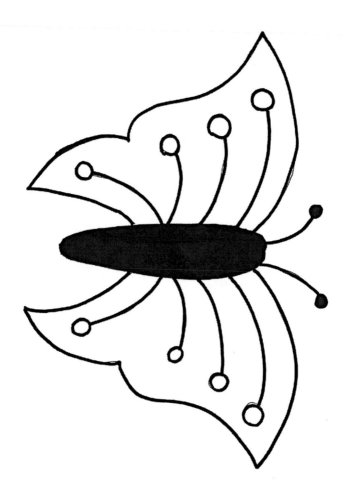

**The Butterfly
(Resurrection)**

48

**The Crown**
**(Eternal Life)**

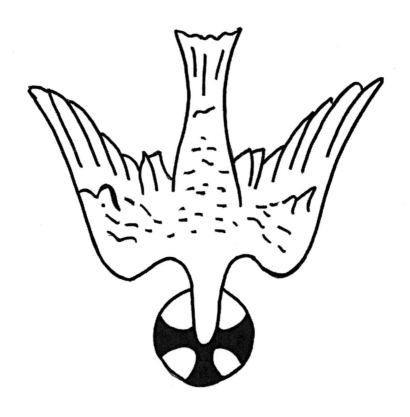

**The Dove**
**(The Holy Spirit)**

50

**The Flame**
**(The Holy Spirit)**

51

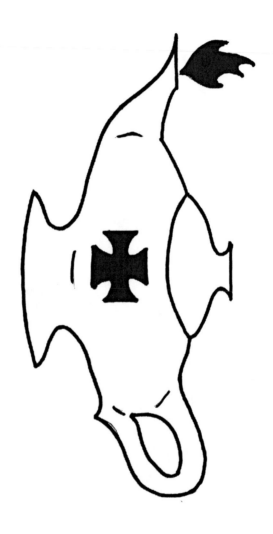

**The Lamp**
**(The Word)**

52

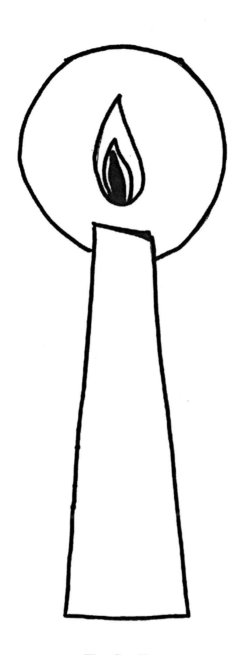

**The Candle**
**(The Word)**

**The Shell**
**(Our Baptism)**

**The Chalice**
**(Holy Communion)**

**(Kneeling Servant)**

CPSIA information can be obtained at www.ICGtesting.com
Printed in the USA
BVOW03s1113270813

329500BV00008B/165/P